Bully

Harassment of Adults

A Resource for Employees, Organisations and Others

**To the Point
Transformational Handbooks
for Business and Personal
Development**

 PUBLISHING

To the Point

Copyright © Jacqueline Mansell 2017
ISBN 978-0-9956296-6-0
A CIP catalogue record
for this book is available from the British Library
First printed 2017
Published by FCM PUBLISHING
www.fcmpublishing.co.uk

Dedicated to
Ted

To the Point

Contents

Part 1.

Understanding human behaviour.

A general overview

Part 2.

Seeing the bigger picture.

Exploring the links between harassment and
bullying with prejudice and discrimination.

Recognizing that harassment and bullying is on a continuum of behaviors

Part 3.

Recognizing harassment and bullying

Part 4.

Understanding those who bully and harass and
their wider impact

Part 5.

Why you?

Making sense of being bullied and harassed.

Introduction
Bullying and Harassment of Adults

Bullying and harassment can be observed in many settings. For example, there have been a number of recent cases reported in residential and care homes, and investigations have been made with respect to those serving in the armed forces. There are many incidents of bullying reported in education and who could ignore the rise of internet trolls singling out complete strangers. Sadly, even reports of neighbours waging campaigns are not unheard of and even the home and family hold no sanctuary for some.

Bullying is not only a problem for those who directly experience it or for those on the peripheries but is a problem for wider society. When society at large tolerates bullying and harassment, the bar is set for all citizens from the young to the old.

This book has been written to examine different facets with respect to bullying and harassment: It begins by developing an understanding of general behaviour. The book then recognises the links that prejudice and discrimination can have with bullying and harassment and identifies how behaviour is on a continuum with potential for a wider impact on society. Next, insight is gained by recognizing and understanding bullying and harassment and the effects upon individuals and organisations. The handbook closes with ideas to support victims of bullying/harassment in overcoming their experience and moving forward.

This book considers bullying and harassment against the background of the workplace setting. It is particularly focussed on individuals who have been or find themselves subject to unwanted behaviour for research has indicated that a significant number of UK employees have experienced some sort of harassment.

Bullying and harassment can involve anyone connected with the workplace:
+ Line Managers
+ Colleagues
+ Agency Workers
+ Customers
+ Suppliers

Bullying can take place downward, upward, peer to peer, from groups or from the organisation.

The handbook presents information suitable to assist those who have been or are subject to bullying and harassment it is also a useful guide for line managers and others who have a role and responsibilities in creating effective and successful organisational cultures.

For organisations and line managers, the aim of this handbook is to:

- Heighten understanding and awareness about the dynamics of groups and individual behaviour in order to address and eliminate bullying and harassment
- Prompt thinking about organisational and team behaviours with a view to promoting a culture which carries the mark of respect
- Eliminate bullying and harassment and generate an environment which is positive, effective and productive

For individuals who have found/find themselves treated unfairly, the aim of this handbook is to gain insight and strength and make sense of what is happening or what has happened by:

- Being aware of the factors that drive behaviour
- Increasing knowledge of bullying and harassment in its widest sense

- ♦ Understanding that the experience can be overcome which can lead to a higher level of personal empowerment
- ♦ Provide a 'tool box' to help on the journey

Please note that while this book is largely set against the background of the workplace, it contains valuable information suitable to other organisations and will be of help to anyone managing others or individuals who are supporting someone who is experiencing or dealing the consequences of harassment and bullying.

About To the Point

'To the Point' are publications, which have been developed and written with different readers in mind, but in all cases designed for practical and easy use. Utilising bullet points, these quick to read handbooks encapsulate experience and knowledge drawn together throughout a career supporting the development of individuals and organisations.

The handbooks provide you with straightforward access to theories, ideas and frameworks proven to achieve results, account for behaviour and which can be integrated into everyday living.

'To the Point' is ideal for:
- Individuals who would like to increase their personal knowledge and understanding
- Organisations who wish to provide tool books for managers and teams
- People who want to learn quickly
- Discovering ideas, information and concepts to provide a springboard to deeper study

To the Point

Part One. Understanding Human Behaviour

We are a sum of multiple identities

"There is always someone asking you to underline one piece of yourself…whether it's black, woman, mother… because that's the piece they need to key into. They want to dismiss everything else."

Audre Lorde

The facts and figures surrounding incidence of bullying, harassment and discrimination often reduce individuals to a single identity but adults are a complex sum of many identities related for example to:

- Position/role in the family
- Position/role in the community
- Age
- Ethnicity
- Sexuality
- Occupation
- Employment status
- Hobbies
- Interests
- Cultural values, standards and traditions
- Gender
- Marital status
- Religion
- Beliefs
- Values
- Abilities
- Tastes and preferences
- Able bodied / differently abled

- Origin and background
- Ancestry
- Heritage
- The desire for personal change

If you permutated any of the list shown above with the addition of your own unique characteristics and identities, it can be seen that that none of us is limited by the boundaries and labels of a single identity.

The mantle of identities that combine to envelop and create adults is probably immeasurable. We are a collection of multiple identities.

Part One. Understanding Human Behaviour

A general overview of the factors that influence behaviour

"It is not our differences that divide us, it is our inability to recognise accept and celebrate those differences."

Audre Lorde

Behaviour is controlled and moderated due to a combination of many factors:

- Our human biology
- Mental state/capacity
- Our social world/experiences
- Motivating and restraining influences
- Group behaviours and the 'evidence of the crowd'
- Our own sense and strength of moral agency (personal control in regulating and managing our own behaviour in a way that is ethical, right and humane)

- Our Human Biology. Some relevant aspects of the **biological dimension**
  - ❖ The effects of chemical stimulants for example, alcohol or non-prescribed drugs
  - ❖ The 'Selfish Gene' (survival of the fittest & competitiveness)
  - ❖ Hormonal changes & imbalances (For example, levels of Testosterone in both men and women)

- Our Mental State/Capacity. Some relevant aspects related to the **mental component:**
  - ❖ Level & types of intelligence – may not understand the consequences of actions
  - ❖ Emotional intelligence
  - ❖ Empathy - may lack the mental capacity to see how things are for other people
  - ❖ Ability to contextualise, comprehend and rationalise

- Some examples of **social/experiential factors:**
  - ❖ Upbringing/learned behaviour.
  - ❖ Social class
  - ❖ Race
  - ❖ Religion
  - ❖ Sexuality
  - ❖ Marital status
  - ❖ Generational aspect and where an individual is on the timeline in relation to others.
  - ❖ Travel

- ❖ Life experiences. For example, may have experienced conflict and war
- ❖ Culture. For example, as a consequence of nationality, region, community, neighbourhood
- ❖ Experience, type and level of education
- ❖ Experience of work. For example
  - Position at work
  - Level of autonomy
- ❖ Travel
- ❖ Life experiences. For example, may have experienced conflict and war

"People have one thing in common: they are all different."

Robert Zend

Part One. Understanding Human Behaviour

Factors that have a motivating effect upon behaviour

"The time is always right to do what is right."

Martin Luther King Jr.

These are some factors related to those conditions that have a **general motivating role**:

- ♦ The timing of events
- ♦ The circumstances or situation in which events take place
- ♦ Beliefs:
  - ❖ Beliefs are those opinions and convictions held to be true or real even without proof.
  - ❖ People hold beliefs about the world and about themselves. For example, politics and religion
- ♦ Habits:
  - ❖ Are largely formed as a result of past experience
  - ❖ Become routine behaviour over time
  - ❖ Are often carried out without conscious awareness, to the point that people are sometimes unaware that they have formed a habit or find it difficult to break the habit
- ♦ Learned behaviour:

❖ This is behaviour where we have the insight to apply something learned to new situations.

❖ Learned behaviour may also provide us with a reward. For example: Our behaviour provides pleasure or satisfies a need.

❖ The reward may also be the removal of negative circumstances such as mitigating against loneliness, fear of 'losing face' or fear of 'being on the outside' and not being part of a group (which, for example, is why people subject themselves to initiation ceremonies)

❖ Conversely, learned behaviour can help in avoiding 'punishment'. For example: a fear of failure may prevent action or a fear of the consequences (punishment/pain). *(The avoidance of punishment can be observed when people are driving, it is why traffic cameras slow us down).*

♦ Factors related to **satisfying biological and intrinsic need**s (as identified by the psychologist **Abraham Maslow** who wrote A Theory of Human Motivation) This is behaviour in response to the environment and to meet our human needs. For example, to:

❖ Satisfy our basic needs such as keeping a roof over our head or having food to eat

❖ Protect ourselves from threats, physical attack and danger

❖ Maintain our sense of belonging. We may desire or seek out affection, friendship or love or have the need to feel a sense of connection to others by being part of a group. (In doing this we may ensure that we 'don't rock the boat', 'go along with the crowd' or try to avoid ridicule or negative attention)

❖ Gain the esteem of other people (In doing this some people might 'put others down' manipulate others or misuse power)

- ❖ Achieve our highest potential
- ❖ Meet the needs that go beyond our own self-interest which includes achieving truth and justice (described by Maslow as 'Meta Needs')

♦ **The 'Evidence of the Crowd'**

People may be motivated by 'The Evidence of the Crowd' which means that behaviour and ideas are shaped and moderated by the behaviours of others:

- ❖ With whom the individual identifies
- ❖ During times of uncertainty
- ❖ When ambiguity or doubt prevails
- ❖ In the search for norms of group behaviour

Hence why people conform and don't take action despite facts in front of them

♦ The 'Evidence of the Crowd' can have a powerful effect upon moderating and motivating behaviour. Individuals may:

- ❖ Go along with the crowd
- ❖ Suppress doubts
- ❖ Take a 'blinkered view'
- ❖ Demonstrate compliance by publicly accepting views while privately despising or rejecting them
- ❖ Avoid standing out so as to negate negative attention or the ridicule of others
- ❖ Avoid argument in order 'not to create waves' and to maintain harmony (sometimes also found in the phenomenon identified as 'Group Think')
- ❖ Rationalise the ideas of other members of the group
- ❖ Take a position whereby they want to show sensitivity to the opinions and the actions of others around them
- ❖ Fail to offer alternatives

❖ Make the assumption that since everyone else is doing something it is okay to do the same

❖ Accept the group norms in order to identify and maintain a relationship that is self-defining

❖ Positively internalise and adopt behaviours because they are consistent with personal values and beliefs

By being part of the crowd the normal standards of behaviour are justified as a trait of the group rather than the standpoint of any particular individual group member.

The 'Evidence of the Crowd' enables a person to stand outside of themselves and so become an object free from personal restrictions and responsibility.

Counter-conformity

While people may be motivated by 'The Evidence of the Crowd', conversely there are occasions when people do not conform:

- ❖ Independence and self-sufficiency is valued
- ❖ A person is individualistic and does not want to be seen to be the same as everyone else
- ❖ Being true to 'themselves' is more important than 'fitting in' or belonging to a group
- ❖ A social issue or social justice is so important to an individual that they choose to be in the minority

Part One. Understanding Human Behaviour

The power of groups

"An individual in a crowd is a grain of sand, amid other grains of sand, which the wind stirs up at will."

Le Bon

Membership and a sense of belonging to a group has a powerful effect upon individual wellbeing and on organisational/institutional achievement. From the earliest times in human history, the cooperation of individuals in social groups has enabled people to build sustainable communities through to creating the global networks we see today.

- Group membership can generate a sense of:
    - Belonging
    - Self-worth
    - Dedication
    - Purpose
    - Security
    - Protection
    - Attachment

- Group membership can:
    - Fill an 'existential vacuum' and give

life meaning

❖ Reduce boredom

❖ Provide parameters and structure for living

❖ Provide a framework which absolves the need to make decisions

♦ Even the largest groups provide people with the sense that they share common membership and association with others. Consider the following:

❖ Neighbourhoods

❖ Regions

❖ Countries

❖ The organisations that people work in or belong to

❖ School/College/University

❖ Following a sport or being part of a team. For example, football and cycling

❖ Religions

❖ Fans of celebrities

❖ Sisterhood/brotherhood

❖ Political affiliation

♦ The bonds of belonging to a group may not be directly developed as a consequence of contact between individuals but through the representation, symbolism and bonds that identifies membership:

❖ Celebrities

❖ Ambassadors for the group

❖ Images

❖ 'Inherited' ideas and knowledge

❖ Beliefs (that provide the reason for being part of the group)

❖ Ideology (ideas) that reflect beliefs

❖ Shared values

❖ Culture

❖ Leaders (who take the place of emotional caregivers). For example:

> Religious leaders
>
> Political leaders
>
> Royal representatives
>
> Business or organisational leaders
>
> Sports Managers/Coaches

♦ By default, an in-group creates an outgroup. Outgroups may be regarded as:

❖ Competition

❖ A threat

❖ A drain on resources

❖ An entity to be feared

♦ On the other hand, where a group is certain and secure, an outgroup is less likely to generate negativity

Part Two. Seeing a bigger picture

Prejudice and Stereotyping

"What others marked as flaws or disadvantages about myself – my race, my gender – I embraced as fuel for success."

Serena Williams

A definition of **Prejudice:**

- ◆ Judgement formed before or without due examination

A definition of a **Stereotype:**

- ◆ A fixed, conventional representation

The reasons for the existence of prejudice and stereotyping:

- ❖ Ignorance
- ❖ Hearsay
- ❖ Past experience
- ❖ Mimicry
- ❖ Superstition
- ❖ Chauvinism (a belief in the superiority of own sex, race etc.)
- ❖ Power (the need to align with power or to submit to power)
- ❖ The aggression of authoritarian persons

- ❖ Projectivity:

  > An individual holds what they regard to be undesirable impulses that cannot be admitted and so projects their frustrations onto minorities

  > An individual develops what they consider to be a perversion so disgusting to the self that they project their disgust on to someone else

- ❖ Social conformity. For example, the influences of:

  > Parents

  > The Media

  > Schooling

  > Peer groups and other groups

  > The need to 'fit in' and belong

Part Two. Seeing a bigger picture

Unconscious Bias & Discrimination

"Never look down on anybody unless you're helping him up."

Jesse Jackson

Prejudice and stereotypes can lead to unconscious cognitive bias and discrimination.

The notion of cognitive psychological bias entered the lexicon in the 1980's after studies carried out in the 1970's. There exist many different types of unconscious cognitive bias some of which reinforce prejudice and stereotypes and lead to discrimination.

Bias

- Bias - The Anchoring Effect
  - Intuitive thinking which gives too much weight to past experience/events and not enough to other factors
  - Bias created by first impressions which subconsciously hook into previous thoughts/experience (This is sometimes known as the Halos and Horns Effect, whereby

Confirmation Bias is deployed in thought and deed)

❖ Fixing thoughts based upon the first information received instead of substantiating thinking and ideas with information from different sources

♦ Confirmation Bias

❖ Only using information that supports what we already believe

❖ Weighing one piece of evidence too heavily when making choices and decisions

❖ Acting as to ensure confirmation bias is proven. For example, a Line Manager having an individual on their team who they dislike so giving them or asking them to do that which they know is not achievable and hence 'confirming' their view that the employee is incompetent

❖ 'Cherry picking' evidence and ignoring anything to the contrary

❖ Surrounding self with 'Yes Men'

❖ Confirmation Bias is observed in the phenomenon identified as the Self-fulfilling Prophecy

♦ Self-Consensus Bias

❖ Only interacting with those people who have the same beliefs and so reinforcing and strengthening personal bias

❖ Sub-conscious leanings

❖ Engagement with things we like more than dislike

❖ Doing things without any reasoning why

♦ Present Bias

❖ Acting without thinking of the consequences or future effects

Discrimination – A definition

Where person A treats person B less favourably than s/he would treat others

The Self-fulfilling Prophecy

Discrimination can lead to a Self-fulfilling Prophecy. In other words, if there is an expectation (at a conscious or a sub-conscious level) that individuals are likely to behave in a certain way, two things may happen:

❖ Onlookers and others might so influence events as to make predictions come true.

For example, single out individuals for particular treatment, prejudice and discrimination

❖ Those individuals who have been categorised as behaving in a certain way may internalise the messages as a frame of reference and so begin to act according to the predictions. For example, the person repeatedly given the message *'You'll never amount to anything'* may accept that they are useless and develop a low sense of self worth

Prejudiced Discriminator

❖ This is the person who holds prejudices and actively acts upon those beliefs

Prejudiced Non-discriminator

❖ This is the person who is prejudiced but does not act on his/her beliefs

Non-prejudiced Discriminator

❖ This person does not hold particular prejudices but either acts as a bystander or joins in with discrimination due to peer group or other pressure, out of fear or in a desire to be part of a group

Non-prejudiced Non-discriminator

❖ This person never has any preconceived ideas or treats others differently

"*Let me not judge another until I have walked in his Moccasins.*"

Native American Prayer

Part Two. Seeing a bigger picture

Discrimination in Action

Allport's Scale of Prejudice

"Those who can make you believe absurdities can make you commit atrocities."

Voltaire

Allport's Scale of Prejudice

In 1954 the American Psychologist Gordon Allport developed a scale of prejudice which identified how levels of prejudice, stereotyping and discrimination can escalate and manifest in society.

Stage 1. This is the phase Described by Allport as **Antilocution.** This is the step that sets the stage for prejudice and is likely to include:

- ❖ Damaging and derogatory discourse or conversation
- ❖ 'Learned' books and writings presenting ideas as 'fact'
- ❖ 'Alternative facts'
- ❖ Hateful opinions
- ❖ Propaganda
- ❖ Dialogue in terms of negative stereotypes. For example, 'jokes', stories, sectarian songs

- ❖ Negative images
- ❖ Depictions in the arts, movies and popular culture
- ❖ Degrading images such as pornography
- ❖ Campaigns and protests
- ❖ The use of social media

Stage 2. Avoidance This is the stage that creates social isolation:

- ❖ People keeping a social distance
- ❖ Rebuffing friendships
- ❖ Ignoring neighbours
- ❖ Preventing marriage within families
- ❖ Preventing employment in a place of work
- ❖ Declining visitors to the country
- ❖ Refusing citizenship

Stage 3. Discrimination Putting prejudice into action:

- ❖ Assuming that somebody has less knowledge or capability due to characteristics e.g. age, gender, race etc.

- ❖ Assuming a hierarchy of power

- ❖ Denying equal access to opportunities such as goods, services, employment

- ❖ In some cases, discrimination may present itself as benign such as treating people like 'pets', being condescending or never seeking their opinions

- ❖ Preventing people from having power by ensuring that they cannot vote or hold official office

- ❖ Creating social disadvantage

- ❖ Acting with the intention to harm by preventing people from achieving their goals, gaining employment, getting an education etc.

Stage 4. Physical Attack

- ❖ Graffiti

- ❖ Vandalism

- ❖ Theft

- ❖ Damage to property

- ❖ Posting faeces, rubbish or other obnoxious things through the victim's letter box

- ❖ Attempted arson or arson

- ❖ Spitting

- ❖ Assault

- ❖ Violence

- ❖ Beating

- ❖ Sexual violence

- ❖ Rape

- ❖ Lynching

- ❖ Atrocities, torture and acts of extreme cruelty

Stage 5. Extermination

- ❖ Destruction

- ❖ Abductions

- ❖ Mass summary executions

- ❖ 'Ethnic cleansing'

- ❖ Actions to ensure the eradication of people and existence of cultures

"Freedom is never more than one generation away from extinction."

Ronald Reagan

Part Two. Seeing a bigger picture

Discrimination in Action

Albert Bandura
Moral Disengagement

"The only thing necessary for the triumph of evil is for good men to do nothing."

Edmund Burke

Why people behave in ways that are inhumane

Psychologist Albert Bandura notably conducted research using a stuffed 'Bobo' doll to show aggressive responses in children. He has presented extensive research about **why people behave** in ways which are at odds with what would be described as normal, humane and moral standards of behaviour including work on modern warfare. From his work we might extrapolate some thoughts with respect to bullying and harassment.

- ♦ **Displaced Responsibility**. Examples include:
  - ❖ *'Just following orders'*
  - ❖ Implicit agreements where accountability is diminished. This means that those 'in the loop' indirectly collude but there is no way in which anyone can be incriminated. Harmful or immoral conduct is muffled and not acknowledged.

❖ Organisational structures which allow for blame to be treated as someone else's responsibility

♦ **Diffusion of responsibility**. For example:

   ❖ Group decision making (*'When everyone is responsible, no one feels responsible'*)

   ❖ Subdividing roles so that individuals are divorced from end results. For example:

In the workplace, bureaucracy such as workplace manuals can reduce procedures into parts and so for example, may not reflect individual experience.

With respect to bullying and harassment, while they may not be consciously subdivided, the small part that each individual might take within a group can have a devastating effect upon the victim meaning that 'The whole is greater than the sum of the parts'

❖ Hierarchical systems and chains of command so that individuals are removed from outcomes. For example:

In the case of bullying and harassment, some organisations have outsourced or other arrangements in place with respect to HR/Personnel which means that there may be a lack of continuity or individuals are separated from the situation

◆ **Impersonalization and Dehumanising People.** For example:

❖ It is easier to depersonalise someone if they are a stranger than if a relationship exists (think of internet trolls)

❖ Reducing others to sub groups, out groups, the other

❖ No longer viewing people as human instead regarding them as *'pigs'*, *'savages'*, *'degenerates'*

- **Disregarding or Distorting Consequences**. For example:
    - ❖ *'Out of sight, out of mind'* For some perpetrators, if they do not hear and see the pain and suffering of others it is easier for them to inflict misery

- **Moral Justification**. Making the case that behaviour normally regarded as unacceptable is right because it is justified on the grounds that it is:
    - ❖ Standing up to oppressors
    - ❖ Preserving values and beliefs

This might be regarded as a double edged sword; on the one hand it might be argued that actions are in the interests of the greater good when on a wider scale we hear of justifications for activities considered as torture.

In cases when people have been bullied or harassed they may want strong retaliation and for the perpetrator to *'learn a lesson'*, to be severely punished through job loss or receive public admonishment through reputational damage

♦ **Sanitising Language**. This acts to downplay behaviour. For example:

❖ The word *'banter'* becomes a euphemism for making harassment acceptable

❖ *'Reallocating resources', 'rightsizing', 'streamlining', 're-engineering',* are words and phrases which disguises the anxiety of those whose jobs are on the line

❖ *'Locker room talk'* suggesting a 'safe space' for crude language towards others

❖ *'Just being one of the lads'* an excuse for someone who causes offense or harm

When considering Allport's Scale of Prejudice and the work of Bandura it is easy to see how bullying and harassment can arise. For example,

- Some men regarding women as inferior to men
- Organisations where transparency is distorted and decisions are 'made in corridors' or to use an old phrase 'smoke filled rooms'
- Vicarious bullying where conflict is created through the deception of manipulative individuals who let *others do the dirty work'*.

Part Two. Seeing a bigger picture

Discrimination in Action

Oppression

Oppression

The injustice, deprivations and abuse of prejudice, stereotyping and discrimination have the power to subjugate individuals and groups which may lead to the following sequence of events:

Repression

❖ Try to suppress and keep the pain and anger of what is happening out of mind

❖ Discouraged from expressing emotion

❖ Keeping feelings under control by bottling them up

❖ Put restraints on any naturally expected response

Depression

❖ Feelings of inadequacy are engendered

❖ Hopelessness

❖ Despair

As a consequence of being in a state of repression and depression, individuals and groups will adopt different responses:

Internalise the oppression

- ❖ Adopt or copy the stereotypes
- ❖ Suffer problems with mental health
- ❖ Blame self or others for the oppression

Submit to the oppression

- ❖ Endure the oppression
- ❖ Try to maintain the status quo
- ❖ Suffer problems with mental health
- ❖ Blame self or others for the oppression
- ❖ Suffer isolation

In trying to find a way out, the oppressed can become an oppressor

- ❖ Manipulated or invited to join the

oppression of others

❖ Acts to join the oppression of another group for survival

❖ Justifies and adopts the stereotypes of another group to create a feeling of personal superiority

In trying to find a way out, the oppressed may fight back

❖ Vengeance

❖ Retaliation

A change in conditions can counter oppression:

❖ The heightened self-awareness, moral agency and actions of individuals who remain sensitive to human suffering and refuse to comply or 'join in'

❖ Policy

❖ Laws

- ❖ Re-education
- ❖ Forgiveness

Awareness Check

Remedies towards creating respect

A basic checklist for organisations

"What counts in life is not the mere fact we have lived. It is what difference we have made to the lives of others that will determine the significance of the life we lead."

Nelson Mandela

In some organisations it is accepted that bullying is just a part of organisational life.

Generally, employers are liable for acts of bullying and harassment of employees in the course of their work. In addition, liability can also be extended to situations where the employer has no direct control over other people but where there should have been reasonable foresight in assessing risks with respect to the welfare of individuals:

♦ **Institutionalized Discrimination** arises where intentional or unintended prejudice, systematic behaviours and thoughtlessness pervades organisations. Normality centres around both explicit and implicit assumptions, attitudes, actions, language and behaviours often explained with phrases such as: *'It's the way things have **always been done** around here'* and *'It's the* *way* ___we___ *do things and it will continue to be the way we do things'*

However, as Bandura states institutionalised discrimination can take a *'heavy toll on its victims'* and points out that it is enabled by social justification, attributions of blame and impersonalised practices. Impersonalised practices may include bureaucracy and activities which lead people to behave in anonymous and impersonal ways. With these points in mind, consider the following:

- ❖ Does everyone in the organisation experience the workplace in the same way?
- ❖ Is there a sense that the organisation is about 'survival of the fittest'?
- ❖ Does consultation take place or are employees threatened with changes

to conditions with the attitude *'If you don't like it you know what to do'*

❖ Have you noticed patterns in staff retention, such as certain groups leaving after only a short time?

❖ Does the organisation experience high rates of staff turnover? Sickness absence? Incidence of stress? Use of grievance and disciplinary procedures? Requests for ill-health or early retirement?

❖ What safeguards are in place to mitigate against the misuse of power? For example, are there mechanisms, checks and balances in place to moderate power? Is power spread out across the organisation?

♦ The 'Implied' Contract and other explicit

Contracts. Codes of Practice and Corporate Code of Ethics:

- ❖ How are values and beliefs communicated?

- ♦ Policy Statements with respect to Bullying and Harassment and respecting dignity
  - ❖ Are they in place?
  - ❖ How often are they monitored and reviewed?
  - ❖ How are they communicated, does regular training take place and how frequently is this carried out? (*Once during the induction period is insufficient*)

- ♦ Procedures for dealing with complaints
  - ❖ Are both formal and informal procedures in place?

❖ Are all employees familiar with the procedures?

❖ Can individuals be confident that they can bring complaints without fear of reprisal?

❖ What are the time scales for dealing with and resolving complaints?

❖ What actions are applied after procedures have been implemented?

♦ **Remember that when an individual has surrendered to unwanted behaviour it does not mean that it was conduct that was welcomed**

♦ To provide focus:

❖ Consider what would happen if the media got hold of a story about your organisation, how would they report it?

❖ Would there be any acceptable justification to outside bodies such as suppliers, customers and others for permitted behaviour?

❖ How would permitted behaviour be regarded if considered by a tribunal of strangers making judgement?

♦ Think about the approach you are taking:

❖ Rather than saying *'Why bother doing this?'* ask *'In what way do we do this?'*

❖ Go beyond what you should be doing and consider **what you could be doing**

Quick Points

Case Study
The Storage Yard

This is a fictitious case study created
to develop awareness and identify some useful points

As a particularly demanding and stressful day draws to a close at the Storage Yard a highly skilled and productive worker explodes into temper because he has arrived back at the site to find that a much wanted cuppa can't be made for him. He has a reputation for being a 'grafter' and while he can be regarded as arrogant and sometimes uncivil he has worked with the company for many years and is known by the boss and others to get stuck in and get the job done. He has been working a long shift (since 6 am) with only a short break and is now told by one of the office staff that the kettle can't be used because it is leaking water, is a health and safety risk and won't be replaced until tomorrow morning because they have been too busy to sort it out. This is too much for the worker who snaps. He grabs his colleague and eyeballs him while forcibly pushing him against a wall and enters into a tirade of foul language, racist and personal abuse.

This has been a tipping point: Given his reputation the worker figures *'they need me more than I need them'*. None the less he has had enough of the place and walks out.

The organisation has turned a blind eye and the worker has never seen a problem with his use behaviour and use of racist language Later on, his former colleague makes a claim for personal injury and racial discrimination which is managed by the company with a confidential settlement and a requirement to sign a confidentiality agreement.

Some Quick Points

✓ Allport's Ladder describes how discrimination can escalate. This case study provides a microcosm: An assumption of perceived power (as an indispensable employee), an assault using strong and racist language which would not be expected to be heard on a one-to-one basis between men in the workplace, finally compounded by a physical assault.

✓ No matter how valuable your employee is, you risk their behaviour escalating if it isn't nipped in the bud. Furthermore, letting behaviour persist sends a message of what is perceived to be okay in terms of acceptable conduct. Had such a case gone forward, the company would likely have been scrutinized with respect to vicarious liability.

"*Anger is an acid that can do more harm to the vessel in which it is stored than to anything on which it is poured.*"

Mark Twain

Part Three. Recognising Harassment & Bullying

Definitions and differences

Harassment

The Equality Act 2010 defines harassment as follows:

Unwanted conduct related to a relevant protected characteristic, which has the purpose or effect of violating an individual's dignity or creating and intimidating, hostile, degrading, humiliating or offensive environment for that individual.

In addition, the Equality Act 2010 identifies key characteristics which are protected by law under the Act. These are called Protected Characteristics.

- ◆ The Protected Characteristics are
    - ❖ Age
    - ❖ Disability
    - ❖ Gender reassignment
    - ❖ Marriage and Civil Partnership
    - ❖ Pregnancy and Maternity *(N.B Harassment applies to all protected*

characteristics except for Pregnancy and Maternity, where any unfavourable treatment may be considered discrimination)

❖ Race

❖ Religion or belief

❖ Sex

❖ Sexual orientation

♦ **Important points** relating to harassment under the act

   ❖ It is not the intention of the perpetrator that is key to deciding whether harassment has occurred but whether the behaviour is unacceptable or disadvantageous by normal standards

   ❖ Complainants of harassment need not possess relevant protected characteristics. It may be that they are wrongly perceived to have or are treated as if they do have a protected characteristic

❖ Harassment may be defined because of an association with a person who has a protected characteristic

Protection from Harassment Act 1997 protects persons from harassment by stating:

A person must not pursue a course of conduct –

a) which amounts to harassment of another, and

b) which he knows or ought to know amounts to harassment of the other

The person whose course of conduct is in question ought to know it amounts to harassment of another if **a reasonable person** in possession of the same information would think the course of conduct amounted to harassment of the other.

A person whose course of conduct causes another to fear, on at least two occasions, that violence will be used against him is guilty of an offence if he knows or ought to know that his course of conduct will cause the other so to fear on each of those occasions.

Bullying

The Arbitration Conciliation and Advisory Service (ACAS) defines bullying has follows:

Offensive, intimidating, malicious or insulting behaviour, an abuse of power or misuse of power through means that undermine, humiliate, denigrate or injure the recipient.

Some fine distinctions which sometimes exist between bullying and harassment in the

workplace

- Harassment

  - ❖ Is often related to one of the protected characteristics

  - ❖ Can usually be recognised straight away by both the victim and by other people

  - ❖ Is more likely to be evidenced by overtly offensive words and language or even have a physical element

  - ❖ May be conducted as a means to gain the approval of peers

  - ❖ Those who are harassed are often perceived as a fairly easy target

- Bullying

  - ❖ Often anyone will do, especially if they stand out, are competent or vulnerable

❖ Bullying may be subtler than harassment. There can be a build-up of incidents which looked at individually or without any frame of reference would seem to be inconsequential

❖ Bullying can be physical but is likely to manifest by being a predominantly psychological assault. For example, unjust criticism or false allegations about performance

❖ Bullying is often 'dressed up'. For example, ridiculing somebody to the refrain of *'Can't you take a joke? Where's your sense of humour?'* or carried out covertly

❖ The target of a bully is likely to be

regarded as someone to be crushed

Bullying and harassment can be an ordeal that goes on for months or even years and is only brought to the fore when a particular incident becomes the 'final straw' or a tipping point has been reached. In most cases it is the repeated and persistent nature of behaviours that constitutes bullying and harassment. However, it should also be noted that where a single incident such as physical violence is so severe that the victim is left in a state of fear, then such an act may be recognised as bullying behaviour.

IMPORTANT NOTE

This section contains reference to legislation but should be treated as a guide only. Relevant Acts, legislation, regulations directives etc. are continuously reviewed and revised to be fit for purpose. Always consult current information.

"*Courage is rightly esteemed the first of human qualities because, as has been said, it is the quality which guarantees all others.*"

Winston Churchill

Part Three. Recognising Harassment & Bullying

Identifying General behaviours

"*When they go low. We go high.*"

Michelle Obama

Some examples of general behaviours which may be identified as bullying and harassment

◆ Exposing someone to unsolicited or unwanted:

   ❖ Offensive jokes or teasing

   ❖ Offensive language

   ❖ Obscene graffiti and images

   ❖ Obscene gestures

   ❖ Sectarian songs

   ❖ Emblems and flag waving

◆ Putting a person under pressure:

   ❖ Unwanted physical contact

   ❖ Intrusion into personal space and possessions

   ❖ Intrusion by pestering, spying and stalking

   ❖ Pressuring someone to participate

in particular activities

❖ Manipulating

❖ Goading and baiting

❖ Being antagonistic

♦ Humiliation:

❖ Setting someone up to fall

❖ Ridiculing someone

❖ Patronising and belittling

❖ Picking on someone

❖ 'Put downs' and criticism (particularly in public)

❖ Teasing and taunting intended to embarrass

❖ Demeaning someone

❖ Shouting and/or swearing at someone in public

❖ Spreading malicious rumours

❖ Gossiping and slander

❖ Verbally insulting someone

❖ Engaging in insulting behaviour

❖ Statements made as unpleasant asides (but loud enough for the target to hear)

❖ On line abuse

❖ Derogatory multiple e-mails (usually Cc & Bcc)

❖ 'Trolling'

♦ Isolation (The impact of isolation can be so damaging to the human psyche and to people's spirit that it has been/is used as a decisive tool of subjugation and mental torture when placing people in solitary confinement or isolation cells in prisons and other institutions):

❖ Segregation

❖ Exclusion from social activities

- ❖ Non-cooperation

- ❖ Sending someone to 'Coventry'

- ❖ Ignoring someone's presence

- ❖ Ignoring someone's opinion

- ◆ Overt displays of animosity:

  - ❖ Damage to possessions

  - ❖ Actions such as deliberately blocking someone's path or barging into them when walking past

  - ❖ Hostility

  - ❖ Irritability and displays of temper

  - ❖ Raised voice

  - ❖ Threatening (which may be in front of others)

  - ❖ Throwing things with force either at the victim or as display of anger

  - ❖ Violence

Part Three. Recognising Harassment & Bullying

Abuse of power in the workplace

"All cruelty springs from weakness."

Seneca

In addition to the general behaviours identified with respect to harassment and bullying, the workplace can be an environment where **other specific conduct is also to be found:**

- Treating someone differently to others:
  - ❖ Setting unachievable goals and deadlines
  - ❖ Failing to provide the support that is given to everybody else
  - ❖ Denying an individual adequate resources, while other people receive their fair share
  - ❖ Withholding information and knowledge, so making it difficult to achieve results or setting someone up to fail
  - ❖ Subjecting someone to excessive supervision – micro-management

that is not applied to others

❖ Different 'rules' are applied. For example, coming back from lunch a minute late is cause for reprimand while others can flout regulations

❖ Being required to comply with policy, procedure and regulations to the absolute letter, at all times and given no let-up

❖ Requiring checks, examination monitoring and evidence of results which is not required of others

❖ Requests for leave are treated reluctantly, agreed to on a conditional basis or made to be unnecessarily complicated

❖ Jobs are unfairly allocated

❖ Unwelcome sexual advances

- Putting someone under pressure with respect to their workplace role and responsibilities:

  - Responsibilities either remain the same or increase while at the same time levels of authority or staffing are removed

  - Overloading with work

  - Landing someone with work at the close of day or immediately prior to holidays

  - Having position undermined as the function of the role is reduced and replaced with lower status or demeaning work

  - The 'goal posts' are changed. Targets and objectives are altered without reason or as they are near to completion

- Creating bewilderment and confusion:

  - Regardless of possessing necessary qualifications, levels of competence or experience, the victim is constantly having to prove themselves

  - The victim is told that they possess characteristics or display actions totally at odds with reality. For example, told that they are lazy when they are very hard working. Informed they lack creativity when outputs show otherwise

  - Frequently on the receiving end of fault finding and criticism

    on the other hand

  - Work is plagiarised and passed off as belonging to the bully

  - Opportunities for promotion and

> training are blocked for no objective
> or understandable reason

❖ The victim's job description is vague or too demanding

❖ One-to-one communication with the victim is circumvented and instead conducted by such means as e-mail, written notes or through other parties

❖ False accusations are made about the victim

◆ Meetings and other gatherings:

❖ Being undermined in front of others. For example, 'concerns' are publicly raised about work and performance

❖ The victim is publicly reprimanded

❖ The victim is subject to subtle signs

such as lack of eye contact or being side-lined

❖ The victim is disregarded, opinions dismissed, overruled or subject to personal remarks

Part Three. Recognising Harassment & Bullying

Examples of behaviours related to Protected Characteristics

"If you're going through hell, keep going."

Winston Churchill

In addition to the general behaviours and abuse of power identified earlier, the workplace can be an environment where **other conduct** is also to be found **particularly associated with protected characteristics:**

Some additional examples - Sexual bullying / harassment

Sexual harassment can be:

- ◆ A man harassing a woman
- ◆ A woman harassing a man
- ◆ A woman harassing a woman
- ◆ A man harassing a man

- ◆ Verbal:
    - ❖ Being asked intrusive questions about one's sex life
    - ❖ Embarrassing questions about health or references to 'that time of

the month'

- ❖ Being quizzed about what underwear is being worn
- ❖ Inappropriate references to figure/physique
- ❖ Whistles, catcalls
- ❖ Suggestive comments
- ❖ Insults
- ❖ Threats
- ❖ The use of pejoratives such as calling someone *'dearie'*

- ◆ Non-verbal:
  - ❖ E-mails, messages and other communication with a sexual content
  - ❖ Frequently leering or staring at an individual's body
  - ❖ Displaying offensive materials

❖ Suggestive looks or gestures

❖ Sitting or standing too close, encroaching into personal space (the victim finds that they are having to keep edging/moving away)

♦ Physical:

  ❖ Unwelcome sexual advances (touching, squeezing, putting arms around someone, grabbing, patting, pinching, kissing, hugging)

  ❖ Regularly brushing against the victim

  ❖ Assault

  ❖ Attempted rape

  ❖ Rape

♦ Pressure:

❖ Keep asking to meet or go for *'a quick drink/coffee'* or to go on a date even after you have said no

❖ Asking for sexual favours

❖ Arranging for a room to be shared on a business trip

❖ Propositions on the proviso of advancement

❖ Persistently giving unwanted gifts

Some additional particular examples with respect to Racial bullying and harassment

♦ Intolerance, being singled out and/or criticised on the basis of:

❖ Appearance

❖ Customs

❖ Beliefs

❖ The way the victim talks

- Finding reasons not to work with the victim
- Expecting the victim to undertake stereotyped tasks and roles
- Displaying racially offensive material
- Insults and racist 'jokes'
- Being subject to insulting noises and gestures
- Using derogatory names

Some additional particular examples of bullying and harassment based on Disability

- Inappropriate questions about the impact of someone's disability
- The use of patronising and insulting language
- Making fun of someone's appearance
- Under pressure to constantly hide disability and prove self

Some additional particular examples of bullying and harassment based on Sexuality

- Intimate questions about sexuality
- Threats to disclose sexuality

Some additional particular examples of bullying and harassment based on Age

- Excluding someone from activities on the basis of age
- Making assumptions about goals and abilities on the basis of age
- Excluding someone from training on the basis of age
- 'Initiation' ceremonies carried out on young workers
- Humiliating young workers by setting them up with nonsensical tasks or situations

Awareness Check

Remedies towards creating respect

The concept of the Clapham Omnibus

"We must ask ourselves what the man on the Clapham omnibus would think."

Sir Charles Bowen

The notion of the man on the Clapham omnibus is a guideline which was introduced into law in the Victorian era. In essence it poses the question of how a situation would be viewed or thought of by the average man or woman travelling on the bus or in the street, an ordinary, disinterested person who is:

- Informed
- Reasonable
- Fair minded

This principle is a very useful tool for recognising harassment and bullying for when embroiled in difficult situations it can be the case that people get used to and tolerate foibles, behaviours and mores. However, the following questions may provide a useful check for organisations, line managers and individuals:

- Would behaviour fit with how you would want your partner, son, daughter, relative or friend to be treated?

- How happy would you be about the behaviour if it was being carried out in front of other people?

- Given reasonable consideration and in all likelihood, is the behaviour/action as such it would cause offence to any reasonable person, present or not?

- Is regard and respect being shown to the person/people to whom the behaviour/action is directed

- Does the behaviour/action comply with organisational standards, values, Codes of Conduct, Policy and Procedures. legislation?

Part Four. Understanding those who bully and harass and their wider impact

Those who are disposed to bullying and harassment

♦ **Character (Personal Qualities):**

> ❖ Flawed sense of morals. For example, prepared to steal or take the credit for others work
>
> ❖ Deceitful and devious
>
> ❖ Untrustworthy
>
> ❖ Selfish
>
> ❖ A compulsive need to control

♦ **Personality (Innate Traits):**

> ❖ Psychopathic. Unmoved by the distress caused by their decisions and behaviours. Has no remorse and lacks a conscience. Is devious and untrustworthy
>
> ❖ A person who is inwardly directed and doesn't understand the impact of their behaviour on others
>
> ❖ A hedonistic person who seeks

gratification

❖ Narcissistic. Likes to be the centre of attention. For example, engages in dramatics or is over emotional. Alternatively, seeks attention by showing what a great person they are (behind which lies an 'empty shell')

❖ Attention seeker. A clingy person who requires constant support, encouragement, attention or reassurance. If this regard and attentiveness is withdrawn or perceived to be deficient the bully/harasser will turn on the victim

♦ **Learned behaviours:**

    ❖ Emulating behaviours of role

models who are perceived to be successful

- ❖ May not have had a stable background

- ❖ Since childhood have not learned normally accepted standards of behaviour and do not understand the consequences of their conduct

- ❖ Have had a troubled, chaotic childhood and grown up with violence

- ◆ **Self-belief:**

    - ❖ Inferiority complex

    - ❖ Low self-esteem

    - ❖ Low self-confidence

    - ❖ Insecure

    - ❖ Feels inadequate

    - ❖ Fears being found wanting

❖ Fears that failings will be exposed

♦ **Disposition and outlook:**

❖ Prejudiced

❖ Self-interested

❖ Callous

❖ Resentful

❖ Bitter

❖ Jealous

❖ Feels a sense of rejection which has not been overcome

❖ Envious

❖ Hates those people who possess greater levels of knowledge and competence

❖ Hates those people who are more popular

❖ Vengeful (may themselves have been bullied in the past and seek revenge)

- ❖ Spiteful

- ❖ Conciliatory individuals are regarded as pushovers

- ❖ Anyone who ignores the bully/harasser are regarded as a challenge

- ◆ **Behavioural Traits:**

  - ❖ Poor communication skills

  - ❖ Poor language skills

  - ❖ Displays immature behaviour and manners

    conversely

  - ❖ Some bullies are superbly skilled in manipulating communication and twisting an argument with the purpose and outcome of outwitting others during disputes

- ❖ Finds difficulty in acknowledging or praising the contributions, value or achievements of others
- ❖ Criticism is the default position
- ❖ Addicted to bullying and harassment either to alleviate boredom and idleness or because it is thrilling and provides an adrenaline rush
- ❖ Domineering
- ❖ Authoritarian
- ❖ Competitive
- ❖ Arrogant and overbearing believing that they have knowledge and skills which cannot be disputed
- ❖ Lacking in emotional intelligence

but

- ❖ May have high levels of intelligence focused on being cunning, wickedness and even criminality

❖ Possesses a malevolent aura and even a chilling evil stare. Their presence pervades the atmosphere

❖ Behaves as a confident, appearing to be friendly and kind but cannot be trusted. Any personal information, opinions or views disclosed by the victim are used inappropriately, either to publicly undermine or as a weapon to bully

❖ Manipulative. For example, pleasant, charming and convincing in front of some people while out of view 'gas-lighting' or being vindictive and nasty to the victim

on the other hand

❖ Superficially friendly and likable with the victim while behind their back undermining them, belittling them, discrediting, blaming and denigrating them

- ❖ Passive/aggressive. For example, by stealth, they sabotage the victim. They may say they are going to do one thing and then do another.

- ❖ Spreads gossip

- ❖ Back stabbing

- ❖ Able to lie and make things up on the spot

- ❖ Moody

- ❖ Angry and quick tempered

- ❖ If 'buttons' are pushed, resorts to physical attack

Quick Points

Case Study
The Corporate Event

This is a fictitious case study created
to develop awareness and identify some useful points

It is the evening of an annual corporate event which is being held during the run-up to Christmas, giving everyone a chance to relax and to enjoy a drink. The event is attended by approximately 300 employees and their guests. During the dinner a senior staff member, the Divisional Director for Business is going to give a speech.

The event has been going for about two hours when, with all eyes on him the Divisional Director begins his speech. During delivery of the speech the Divisional Director has drawn a lot of laughter and is on a 'bit of a roll' as he spots one of the waitresses clearing tables towards the back of the room. He exaggeratedly licks his lips and says words to the effect of *"There's a pretty little thing. If only I was 20 years younger you'd be going back to my room tonight and wouldn't get out alive. Ha ha" While* people turn to look towards the back of the room the waitress maintains her professionalism and continues her work and takes used crockery back to the kitchen. The speech continues when five minutes later the waitress returns to the room to continue clearing tables. Once again the Divisional Director spots her and says *'She's back again, I must be in with a chance'*.

The waitress confides to her friends that she went home crying and felt utterly humiliated but daren't say anything about the incident because this is her first job and she doesn't want to be seen to be making trouble. None the less, a few days after the event, the Divisional Director is spoken to by the Police about his comments as it emerges that a member of the audience has made a complaint. Subsequently the Crown Prosecution Service (CPS) examines the case.

<u>Some Quick Points</u>

✓ The victim does not have to be the one who makes a complaint as anyone can report it.

✓ The CPS does not act for the victim but 'on behalf of the public and not just in the interests of any particular individuals'.

✓ If you are in a group or with people you consider to be your peers, when making comments it should not be assumed that your peer group will have the same values as you.

✓ 'Jokes' can be regarded as words that are threatening or abusive. It is not a defence to say 'I was only having a laugh'.

"My pain may be the reason for somebody's laugh. But my laugh must never be the reason for somebody's pain."

Charlie Chaplin

Part Four.

Understanding those who bully and harass and their wider impact

Particular modes of bullying

"*When you betray somebody else, you also betray yourself.*"

Issac Singer

Habitual, predatory, serial bullies

Probably the most common type of bullying: Victims of the habitual bully are most likely to simply be in the **wrong place at the wrong time**. In addition to the characteristics and behaviours previously identified, this type of bully:

- Moves from one victim to the other
    - ❖ Uses staff reorganisations as a convenient means to select victims which, by default is likely to conceal the extent of the problem as people move on
    - ❖ Picks off one person after another to be bullied. Individuals anxiously wait for their turn to come around but unlike a roundabout, this is no merry-go-round
    - ❖ New recruits may not stay long and so the behaviour can be repeated

with impunity as people come and go

- May have held a grudge for many years while waiting for the time to act on someone who stands out or who may have unwittingly slighted them etc.

- Like a puppeteer is adept at manoeuvring others around them to carry out their maltreatment. For example,

  ❖ Deploys the individual with whom the bully has manipulated into believing they have a special relationship or the Narcissist, who is seeking attention

  ❖ Plants the seed of ill will towards the victim in the mind of others (see the Self-fulfilling Prophecy). In turn the puppet of the bully, who might for example be the victim's manager carries out functions such as closely monitoring the victim, putting them under pressure or giving them unwarranted criticism

♦ Understands that some organisational structures mean that the business does not have the capacity to adequately address bullying/harassment

♦ Acts in the confidence that the organisation 'turns a blind eye', seeking to avoid investigations and placing a spotlight on the problem

Bullying by groups (also referred to as Gang Bullying and Mobbing) & the role of bystanders

Bullying by groups of people is usually orchestrated by the habitual bully who encourages and creates unacceptable behaviour. This is done either by example or manipulating from the sidelines:

- The victim becomes a scapegoat
- Some individuals adopt the behaviours encouraged by the bully because they are consistent with their own personal beliefs (this is a process known as Internalisation)
- Individuals within the group feel that they have justification for any unpleasant behaviours
- Individuals feel that they are able to 'get away' with conduct that would otherwise be unacceptable because everyone else is doing it
- Some people will feel that they have got no choice but to go along with the behaviour
- Some people will be seen to accept the conduct of the bully and the rest of the group while privately thinking differently
- Some members of the group behave as

bystanders. They may empathise with the victim but will take their cues from the rest of the group (social influence)

♦ Bystanders may feel inhibited from supporting the victim if they are fearful or if they do not want to risk drawing attention to themselves. Bystanders may believe themselves to be helpless or unable to stand up to the group

♦ If alone with the victim, a bystander feeling some responsibility may try to reach out

♦ The need for group belonging takes priority over personal responsibility for the victim which, can be devolved to others

♦ The victim is ostracised and made to feel distress not by one person on many occasions but by many, each only needing to act or standby and do nothing on few occasions

"The obvious is that which is never seen until someone expresses it simply."

Kahlil Gibran

Part Four. Understanding those who bully and harass and their wider impact

The impact of bullying and harassment on organisations

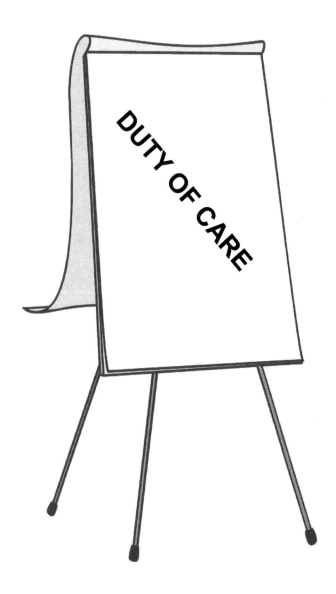

The Organisation

- Financial impact:

    - ❖ On-costs. Additional, non-productive time is spent dealing with the situation

    - ❖ Increased sickness, associated early retirements, staff turnover and recruitment can increase costs to the business

    - ❖ Managing claims, legal fees and settlements

    - ❖ Some organisations are obliged to ensure that legislation is being properly applied before entering into contracts. Therefore, potentially lucrative business could be lost

- Reputational impact:

- ❖ Externally. Information is shared by staff with friends and family leading to damage to the organisation's public image locally (*Who would want to work there!*)
- ❖ Externally. Possible unwanted media attention which can quickly go viral
- ❖ Externally. Suppliers and customers do not want to be associated with the organisation
- ❖ Internally. The reputation and respect for line management and others is eroded

- ♦ Teams:
  - ❖ A change in relationships
  - ❖ An uneasy atmosphere diminishes performance and productivity

❖ The team may become divided

❖ Team members may wish to avoid both the victim and the bully/harasser

❖ The pressures of working in an unpleasant environment may permeate into life outside of work as it becomes a topic of conversation and source of anxiety

❖ Team members may suffer a lack of enjoyment in their job and not want to come into work

❖ After formal procedures have been carried out, working relationships are unlikely to be the same

❖ Good people are lost as both victims and others know that a better working life is to be found elsewhere

"Remember, no one can make you feel inferior without your consent."

Eleanor Roosevelt

Quick Points

Case Study
The Recording

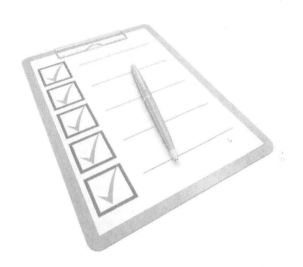

This is a fictitious case study created
to develop awareness and identify some useful points

A state of the art training facility includes an annex which houses special syndicate rooms that are fitted with close circuit TV facilities. The rooms have been equipped for the purpose of making recordings of role play situations in order to review and evaluate behaviour in a systematic and 'safe' training environment.

As the working day begins, two close colleagues who haven't seen each other for a while (as one of them has been on holiday), slip into one of the syndicate rooms for a 'catch-up' and a bit of a gossip. Believing the recording equipment is currently switched off they start to engage in a conversation which turns to racist and derogatory statements about another member of staff. In the meantime, the rest of the team start to arrive and as they enter the main office can both see and hear what is being said.

The two colleagues are subject to disciplinary action.

It latter emerges that there is a short clip of footage which had been captured at the end of a recording some months earlier where one of the perpetrators was engaged in talking to someone else. In this recording both parties were using similar racist tones about team members as had been seen by staff in the main office.

As momentum builds around the situation, additional evidence comes to light which presents another unacceptable exchange by the original perpetrators.

<u>Some Quick Points</u>

✓ Cliques can fuel each other's behaviour. Managers may wish to consider and implement actions to mitigate against the negative elements of exclusive factions.

✓ Evidence that predates disciplinary offences can have a substantial impact. Regardless of any disciplinary action that has taken place, if other evidence comes to light this can still lead to a termination. It could be said that had the organisation known about the new evidence when making its original decision, it would have come to a different conclusion.

✓ In the workplace you are always on duty. It does not matter if you have informal moments behind the scenes or believe that your comments are being made in the security that they are not being heard by other people. When you are at work, making comments in private, i.e. *"The customer never heard me say it"* or *"I said it in my tea break"* is not relevant.

"We shall not be judged by the criticisms of our opponents, but by the consequences of our acts."

Winston Churchill

Awareness Check

Remedies towards creating respect

Workplace Line Management

You will find no modern school of leadership/management that advocates bullying and harassment as an effective management technique.

In addition to the areas previously identified, leaders and line managers can bully and harass because they are:

♦ Working in a dysfunctional organisation which accepts a tacit understanding of conduct or tolerates a hierarchical set of behaviours

♦ Under pressure to achieve results

♦ In a position where they have been over promoted

♦ In a place of fear (being themselves bullied from those above or others seeking returns and outcomes)

♦ Behaving in line with the culture of the organisation

♦ Lacking the capability and competence to

undertake their role

♦ Lacking knowledge and training

Regardless of the circumstances, in most cases, given their position and function line managers should possess sufficient self-awareness to recognise the impact that they have on other people and their personal role and responsibilities in creating a safe working environment. Furthermore, under legislation, line managers have a duty to protect an employee's health as part of their **'duty of care'**

♦ **The organisation should invest in line managers by ensuring that they have the opportunity to complete skills audits, are properly trained and that training is regularly refreshed with respect to:**

  ❖ Up to date people management techniques

❖ Communication skills

❖ Team Building

❖ Personal Stress Management

❖ Respecting Diversity (Including knowledge of organisational policy and relevant legislation)

❖ Health and Safety Risk Management

❖ Grievance and Disciplinary procedures

❖ Workplace counselling

♦ **For those in a line management role, recognize that there is a difference between robust management and bullying**

❖ Undertake change management with care and sensitivity. Uncertainty can unwittingly create a breeding ground for undesirable behaviour

❖ Instead of using the pressure of criticism or sarcasm in response to short falls in the workplace, engage in systematic processes of performance management

❖ Foster harmonious, collaborative and productive team relations by being inclusive, fair and using relevant management techniques

❖ Be observant to the dynamics of the team and act to ensure that staff members do not engage in bullying/harassment

❖ Should incidents or inappropriate conduct come to light maintain impartiality and demonstrate fairness

❖ Do not get into a positon where there is potential for intimidation. Uphold high standards. **Model the way**

♦ **Supporting your team through the experience of bullying or harassment.**

Should you find that a case of bullying or harassment is reported to you it is important that you follow the policies and procedures required by your organisation.

❖ You must be seen as impartial

❖ Maintain normal relations with the victim and the alleged perpetrator

❖ Your approach to the alleged perpetrator should be one of respect. Try not to judge them as they may not have intended or been aware of the impact of their behaviour

❖ Ensure that the team understands the need for confidentiality and understands the actions being taken. Explain the reason, namely to ensure due and proper process

❖ Continue to undertake normal activities such as team meetings

❖ Consult with HR/Personnel should you consider that team members might require counselling during this period

♦ **Rebuilding your team following the experience of bullying or harassment.**

❖ The victim may require counselling to rebuild their confidence, to consider their own behaviour in relation to the bully/harasser and to think about their future

❖ The perpetrator may require counselling to diagnose underlying causes for behaviour and to identify more effective and appropriate behaviour for the future

❖ Any reprisal to any party should be nipped in the bud

❖ Team building may be useful to explore how the situation has impacted upon individuals, what people have learned, to focus on the future and how each will play a part in caring for one another and creating a culture of respect

Part Five. Making sense of being bullied and harassed

Those who are vulnerable to bullying and harassment

"The silence of the envious is too noisy."

Kahil Gibran

◆ **'Tall Poppy Syndrome'. Something about the victim means they stand out:**

> ❖ Different in terms of looks and demeanour
>
> ❖ Good at job
>
> ❖ Popular with people. For example, having the respect and trust of others
>
> ❖ Popular with people. For example, attractive, funny, easy going
>
> ❖ Inadvertently usurped the bully's position as 'top dog' or the centre of attention
>
> ❖ As by comparison to the bully, they have inadvertently exposed the bully's shortcomings such as their inability to carry out their role or their lack of knowledge
>
> ❖ Has stood up to a bully (a definite

predictor of anger and retaliation!)

- ❖ Being the person others go to for advice
- ❖ Refuses to join a clique
- ❖ Prepared to stand by own values
- ❖ Been promoted
- ❖ Publicly recognised or award winning

- ♦ **Character. A person can be vulnerable because they:**

    - ❖ Are incorruptible and have high standards
    - ❖ Believe in being loyal and dependable
    - ❖ Are perfectionists
    - ❖ Go the 'extra mile'
    - ❖ Are helpful and kind
    - ❖ Look to see the good in others

- ❖ Are forgiving

- ❖ Are sensitive

- ❖ Are self-deferential

- ❖ Have an inclination towards passive behaviour

- ❖ Are optimists and idealists

- ❖ Are prepared to make a stand on behalf of others (this character trait may also be expressed by holding a post such as a union rep. or having exposed activity by whistleblowing)

- ❖ Are prepared to 'put their head above the parapet' by giving ideas, opinions or challenging viewpoints

- ❖ Are trustworthy

- ❖ Display integrity

- ❖ Are reasonable and have a strong sense of 'fair play'

- ❖ Are tolerant

- ❖ Avoid saying 'no'

- ❖ Have a 'long fuse' and are slow to provocation

- ❖ Hold their anger in

- ❖ Normally, employ strong coping mechanisms and will only react when a tipping point has been reached

- ♦ **The victim has an area or vulnerability. For example:**

  - ❖ Different because of:

    -Social class

    -Regional accent

    -The school the person went to

    -The neighbourhood in which the person lives

-Factors related to the Protected Characteristics

-Working patterns. For example, Part-Timers being side-lined

❖ May be perceived to lack support networks. For example:

-Alone, single, divorced

-New to the team or organisation

-New to the profession

❖ It is known they fear losing their job due to the burden of commitments such as family and home

❖ Not part of a group

❖ They are perceived as the 'odd one-out'

"It is not what happens to you, but how you react to it that matters."

Epictetus

Part Five. Making sense of being bullied and harassed

The impact of bullying and harassment on the victim

*"Sometimes even to live
is an act of courage."*

Seneca

♦ **Mental health. For example:**

❖ Unable to concentrate

❖ Forgetfulness

❖ Unable to stop thinking about what is happening

❖ Ruminating and soul searching. For example: *'What did I do wrong?' 'What did I do to deserve this?' 'How did I let this happen?'*

❖ Sleep difficulties (including problems getting off to sleep, staying asleep and being awake too early)

❖ Anxiety

❖ Moodiness

❖ Constantly on edge

❖ Over sensitive

❖ A profound dread of going into work

- ❖ Finds the journey to work difficult, maybe having to stop and pull the car over and force self to put on 'a mask' and 'keep a stiff upper lip' ready for the day ahead
- ❖ Worried about the motives of other people
- ❖ Irritability
- ❖ Short tempered
- ❖ Outbursts of anger that are out of character
- ❖ Low self-esteem
- ❖ Feelings of shame
- ❖ Stress
- ❖ Over performing leading to burnout
- ❖ Lack of confidence
- ❖ Depression
- ❖ Suicidal thoughts

♦ **Physical health. For example:**

- ❖ Headaches and migraines

- ❖ Fatigue and exhaustion

- ❖ Constantly tired

- ❖ Loss of libido

- ❖ Feeling faint

- ❖ Heart palpitations

- ❖ Racing heart beat

- ❖ Sweating

- ❖ Panic attacks

- ❖ Eating problems: Eating for comfort or losing appetite

- ❖ Weight gain or weight loss

- ❖ Immune system lowered and so vulnerable to minor illnesses such as colds, throat infections and flu

- ❖ Hair loss

- ❖ Eczema

- ❖ Back and joint pain

- **Normal coping mechanisms are impaired and so the following may occur:**

  - ❖ Resorts to constantly trying to please (be minded whatever you do it will never be enough for the bully)

  - ❖ Retreats into avoidance of others and isolation. For example, by arriving and leaving work either late or early. Avoiding those areas and meeting points frequented by the bully/harasser and so being cut off from teams, groups and individuals. Avoiding social events.

  - ❖ Keeps a low profile with friends and others for fear of having to discuss the situation

  - ❖ Drinking/smoking/drug problems

  - ❖ Comfort found in ways likely to

have a negative impact on a normal lifestyle such as overspending

❖ Beside oneself, crying in private

❖ Bursting into tears at the slightest thing or at inopportune moments

◆ **Working relationships which in the past have been enjoyed are challenged, eroded and impaired:**

❖ The regard of others may be altered as people feel disillusioned or disappointment as they see the victim in an altered light or as a failure

❖ The victim is worried that they will be labelled as a troublemaker if they complain

❖ Because of the manipulative nature of some bullies, the victim is worried that no one will believe them

❖ Some people may distance themselves for fear of being associated with the victim and do not want to become involved

❖ The victim becomes further isolated as colleagues do not want the bully to single them out as the next victim

❖ Some people may find themselves drawn into the unwelcome position of defending the victim creating strained interaction

❖ Sham behaviour may be displayed by some colleagues in simulating sympathy

❖ Colleagues fear being drawn into legal action and so separate themselves from the victim

- ❖ The victim feels self-conscious in front of people who know what is happening or who are likely to have heard rumours and gossip

- ❖ The victim's positivity, contributions and initiative diminish. In meetings the victim may try to become 'invisible', may not offer opinions and simply strive to just *'do as they are told'*

- ❖ Some people may resent the victim, believing that if they had *'Just kept their head down'* or behaved differently the dynamics of the workplace wouldn't have been altered

- ❖ Sickness levels may increase and so colleagues become resentful at having to *'Pick up the slack'*

❖ Being part of the group is more important to people than maintaining a relationship at an individualist level and so the victim becomes an outcast

❖ The victim has been undermined professionally

❖ Some business connections beyond the wider team and immediate work environment may hear about things on the grapevine and consider the victim to be toxic

♦ **Normal supportive relationships are damaged and altered:**

    ❖ The victim feels embarrassed in front of others

    ❖ The victim feels that they have let others down

❖ The people close to the victim feel helpless and frustrated

❖ People closest to the victim feel angry

❖ The victim retreats into silence to avoid upsetting those people around them

or

❖ Talks incessantly about what is happening

❖ The victim feels pressured to be seen to take action which may require great effort (for an individual who by this time has been considerably weakened)

❖ Some male victims may feel that their masculinity has been diminished

❖ Arguments may ensue with the cry

from either party *'I don't want to talk about it!'*

❖ Worries arise with respect to the long term outlook, especially concerns associated with:

> -professional/personal reputation
>
> -taking time off sick
>
> -finances
>
> -potential job loss
>
> -obtaining a reference
>
> -the chances of finding another job
>
> -the prospect of being unable to pay mortgage/rent
>
> -arguments and tensions in a normally loving marriage
>
> -ruining family life and relationships

Part Six. Overcoming the experience of being bullied and harassed

Taking action

Reclaiming your power

At this point you need to muster your strength, and take a rational approach. You will be feeling highly emotional, your professionalism has been undermined and your normal behaviour will be diminished.

- Keep your counsel and do not start a rumour mill (you must at all times be the reasonable party)

- Do not 'badmouth' the bully, colleagues or the organisation

- There is <u>never</u> any excuse for bullying/harassment but first you may wish to consider the following:
  - ❖ Are you being oversensitive?
  - ❖ Do you have 'buttons' that can easily be pushed

❖ Are you overreacting?

❖ Is it the other person who is the problem?

❖ The reasons for the unwanted behaviour: While you should maintain a professional boundary and not allow yourself to be dragged down, is the behaviour because the perpetrator has problems, are stressed or overburdened?

♦ Read guidance compiled by organisations such as The Equality and Human Rights Commission, ACAS and trade unions

♦ Explore what is happening by talking with a trusted individual (someone who will maintain your confidentiality):

❖ Talk through in detail what has been happening (This is going to be difficult as you will be experiencing embarrassment and shame)

❖ Take your time and ponder suggestions. Your disclosure may stir emotions for your confidante. They may feel angry and urge particular ways to proceed. However, the final decision about how you will proceed must lie with you, for once you have decided your course of action it will be you who experiences the consequences

◆ Consider pros and cons and **different ways to approach the situation:**

❖ What do you want to achieve? For the situation to stop

For the situation to stop and receive an apology

For the situation to stop and for the bully/harasser to receive some sort of official redress

❖ Your past record of dependability, service and loyalty may be irrelevant to the current situation. Therefore, would it be a good idea to leave and get another job where you are likely to be valued?

❖ Do you need some respite and have leave of the workplace for a period of time?

❖ Do you want to go down the informal route of talking to the perpetrator and/or writing a letter?

❖ Do you seek 'in-house' mediation (if available within your organisation). (Remember, some bullies regard actions such as mediation as conciliatory with those taking part as being a 'soft touch'. In addition, actions such as the informal process and mediation provide a platform for the manipulatory bully to give the idea that they are irreproachable)

❖ Do you want to go down the formal complaint route of following organisational policies and grievance procedures to address the bullying/harassment?

❖ Are you prepared for Early Conciliation? (Prior to bringing any claim to an employment tribunal you must demonstrate that you have contacted ACAS first, who in turn will act as a broker to help each side come to agreement. All conversations are carried out on a 'without prejudice basis')

❖ Would you feel that you are able to cope with any action leading to an Employment Tribunal?

❖ Is the matter such as it requires Civil Action?

As regards the bully learning a lesson about their own behaviour, this need not be of your concern at this stage. Your mental health and being free of the bully is more important at this time.

Note. In certain situations, the course of action may be out of your hands, particularly in the case of physical assault.

- There may be occasions when a bully/harasser has been lacking in self-awareness. They may:
    - ❖ Not have been aware of the impact of their behaviour
    - ❖ Not have intended or been motivated to cause harm
    - ❖ Simply not care

- Set up a record to document the bullying

and harassment (even if you do not decide to take action at this time you may need this information in the future). Take some time to think back on **everything** that has and is happening:

- ❖ Dates, times, places
- ❖ Note the situation and the context
- ❖ Record what was said and done
- ❖ Keep any corroborating evidence such as e-mails, documents etc.
- ❖ Make a record of any witnesses' present
- ❖ Continue to record incidents as they arise

- ◆ Writing a letter or speaking directly to the bully/harasser.

  Ensure you follow any criteria set out by your organisation and if you feel able (given your emotional state, the nature of the situation, relationship and risks involved) to first of all approach the bully/harasser either in person or with a letter, prepare, think things through and take a step by step approach when presenting the situation:

- ❖ Identify the positives and what you appreciate about the individual
- ❖ Be specific and describe what has been happening
- ❖ Explain the impact and how it is making you feel
- ❖ Let them know that you find the behaviour to be inappropriate, offensive and/or discriminatory
- ❖ Set the bar. Explain your boundaries. Specify what you want to be stopped and what you want to

happen

❖ Explain the benefits of resolving the situation such as a productive working relationship

❖ Seek to obtain agreement in how you can both go forward

❖ Keep a note of the outcome, have things changed for the better or worse?

♦ Escalating the problem to someone in authority such as your line manager may be necessary, in which case:

❖ Describe the things that have been happening

❖ Describe how the situation is having an impact upon your effectiveness in the workplace

❖ If you are aware of other people

having the same experience, alert the listener but be careful not to be seen as trying to persecute the person you are alleging as the bully/harasser

♦ Note, once you have brought the truth of what is happening into the open you may be entering dangerous territory for now the bully may likely see you as the enemy:

❖ The bully will use their guile to lie, charm, dupe and create a different narrative. While given your current mental state, you are likely to appear lame and ineffectual to those parties who do not know you or have not been involved in the situation

❖ The bully may counterattack. This

will put you 'off kilter' as suddenly you are having to deal with new allegations, which in turn detract from the original issues. It is important that you recognise this response has only been made as a consequence of your action and should be treated as being malicious. Furthermore, if the counterattack is not substantiated it can mean that further action with respect to harassment and defamation may ensue

❖ The bully may trivialize or deny that anything of a serious nature has taken place. This is likely to give rise to greater indignation on your part and so could exacerbate the notion that you are the one who is out of control

❖ The bully may claim that they are in fact the victim! Go sick, further confuse you, muddy the process and manipulate others into believing you are the villain of the piece

♦ Take very special care of yourself. You will need all of your strength:

   ❖ Try to eat well

   ❖ Try to get a little exercise

   ❖ You may wish to see your GP

   ❖ Do not withdraw from those people who are supportive. Make an effort to maintain contact

   ❖ If you have lost touch with people, try and reconnect

   ❖ Reduce contact with those people

who sap your energy or who generate a negative vibe

❖ If possible, find a mentor who will provide guidance and help to alter perspective

❖ Absorb yourself in interests/activities which have no association with the organisation

❖ After the working day, try to give yourself some breathing space by going out for a walk or visiting somewhere of local interest

❖ With your work life being unsettled, ensure that your home life is running smoothly. Keep things in the home calm, tidy and organised. In most cases, a home is a sanctuary do not let the situation of bullying and harassment

> pervade your private space
>
> ❖ Do not let yourself go, maintain your personal hygiene and standards
>
> ❖ While at work, have some keepsakes with you such as pocket size items and a few photographs of special people which bring to mind happy memories and invoke good feelings

♦ Whether you have decided to take informal or formal action, identify someone who can help you through the process. Ensure that you follow your organisation's procedures

♦ In the case of Civil action, you will need to contact a solicitor

"Not everything that is faced can be changed, but nothing can be changed until it is faced."

James Baldwin

Part Six. Overcoming the experience of being bullied and harassed

Recovery

Leaving the victim behind

Labelling

Labelling theory argues that by, attaching labels to people, there can be a negative effect upon an individual's power to resolve situations. In other words, if you are told that you are helpless you may adopt that persona.

The concept of the Self Fulfilling Prophecy (as described previously) gives further weight to the notion that, when people are labelled or marked out as possessing particular traits etc. they are likely to elicit reactions and be treated according to the perception of that designation.

To remain under the cloud of being labelled as a victim or described as a survivor creates an implicit relationship, which continues to exist with the bully/harasser. Therefore, recognise:

- ♦ **You were** nothing more than **a target** for

the bully/harasser. Remind yourself that **YOU ARE NOT A VICTIM.** The bully is not worthy of your attention

♦ Sometimes in life there are no immediate logical explanations for events, *'stuff happens'*, sometimes you just happen to have been in the wrong place at the wrong time

♦ Bullies have a keen eye for individuals who perceive themselves as a victim. Therefore, don't give away your power. You are likely to feel exhausted and so don't give the bully any more of your energy or anger by ruminating on events, arm yourself with tolerance

♦ You have gone through a period of fear and anger but reframe your experience, for bizarrely this has been a period of growth for you, while on the other hand (unless the bully's behaviour has been driven by psychosis):

❖ While the bully was engaged in their attempts at hurting you they were acting in accordance with their own internalised pain and weakness. They are likely to keep repeating patterns of behaviour in all walks of their life leading to a downward trajectory

❖ You must have been very important and had a profound impact upon the perpetrator to have held their focus and attention as the selected target

The position of those around you

At this stage, be minded that not all of the people with whom you come into contact will take the same position. Some will:

- Continue to be sympathetic and show loving kindness
- Continue to feel angry about what has happened
- Be disinterested
- Want to engage in and enjoy a bit of scandal and chit-chat
- Push you with probing questions about why you left your job (which may reignite your shame and embarrassment)
- Wonder what it is about you that attracted the attention in the first place, why you didn't stand up for yourself or why you just didn't ignore it (Sympathy and understanding may be low as they may never have been touched by bullying or harassment)
- Experience schadenfreude, secretly taking

a little pleasure in your misfortune

You have remained with the organisation

You may fear that you will be bullied again or that people are against you.

- Try to be rationale and appreciate those who do provide support
- You have been isolated and you may have felt very let down by team members etc. As hard as it is, ensure that you do not withdraw into yourself or become aggressive or surly as this may simply act to confirm some viewpoints
- Whatever the outcome has been of investigations etc. be considered in any encounters with the bully
- Invest in your life outside of the work environment. Engage in interests and activities that give you a different focus

- Recognise that you have enhanced your knowledge and skill and perhaps in time, you could make your experience count (*See the following sections on Post Traumatic Growth & Rebuilding Confidence*)

- If you continue to deal with difficulties or are unhappy, you may want to work to find a better job, one where you are appreciated

You've moved to a new job and it's happening again

Lightening can 'strike twice' but...

- Have an open mind. Be rational, try not to overreact to new situations – pick your battles

- Keep your cool

- In years past when someone felt slighted, the situation could get so out of control it could end up in duel! Keep your control, be rational, ask yourself how much things really matter and what might be the likely outcome of your response

♦ Ask yourself, what's the worst that can happen?

♦ You may see what others cannot see or refuse to see, for as a bully senses a victim, you now understand the dual nature of the bully

♦ You have gained great knowledge, you are wise. In which case you know the recognised sequence of events that is likely to follow. Therefore, you may want to consider the 'price' you pay by staying

Recovering your mettle

It is not always possible or easy to move jobs. For example, some people live in areas with limited opportunities, some people have commitments which might restrict immediate options. Equally, it may be the case that you have weighed up the situation and decided to stay with the current organisation. Whatever the circumstances, this may be a time to ask yourself some questions about your own persona in adapting to the world, a time for analysis and a rational and strategic approach:

♦ Whether in a new or existing workplace, take a realistic view of the environment:

❖ While it is acknowledged that many people meet their life partner at work, it is also important to realise that unless you are working in a family business, the people that you work with are not necessarily your friends. Reframe your thinking about who most individuals are in the workplace from friends to colleagues

❖ Don't attempt to be bosom friends with everyone but one by one build some alliances with trusted individuals

❖ Maintain a professional distance and working relationship, but remind yourself that you are only in the proximity of the people around you, simply by dint of the fact that you happen to have the same employer

❖ 'So what if they don't rate you'. You only have to read things like Trip Advisor, restaurant reviews and other critiques to realise that *You cannot please all of the people, all of the time'*. Ask yourself why you need the approval or validation of people who fail to treat you with consideration or respect? Ask yourself what it is that is important to you about the person who has/is bullying/harassing you? Why is this person important? Are you going to let people intimidate you and if so why?

❖ Trust the opinion of those people who do matter

❖ Armed with the information contained in this book you now understand bullying types, bystanders and behaviours. Therefore, really see things for what they are. While bullying and harassment is never to be condoned, you also know that some perpetrators act from a dark place which may allow you to feel some compassion

❖ While in a toxic environment, maintain your professionalism and focus on your work but while doing so you may wish to imagine yourself in a reinforced, protective suit or bubble. People can see you but they cannot harm you

❖ Remind yourself that everything changes, nothing lasts forever. Staff turnover can alter the dynamics of relationships and alter the organisational culture

♦ Reduce your expectations of how things should be. Not everyone will share your values and standards

♦ Within the context of the environment and without undermining your integrity, ask yourself what is it about you that may not be working and may need to be modified while you bide your time. Think about your posture, tone of voice and the things that you say. Have your strengths become weaknesses?

❖ If you are kind and giving could it be the case that your actions are viewed with suspicion? You may be regarded as untrustworthy. People may wonder why you are doing things and what is in it for you?

❖ If you normally step in to solve problems or speak up could you be seen as overbearing and a busybody?

❖ If you normally say yes, do you need to say no?

❖ Has passivity meant that you are seen as a pushover?

❖ If you are highly knowledgeable do people feel intimidated?

♦ Use someone you admire as a template for moving on. Ask yourself **what would they do** in your situation?

♦ Write a letter to your younger self with advice for the future

♦ Practice control of your emotions. There are many roles that we can use as exemplars where people have to steel themselves for bad situations. For example, Fire Crews rushing towards danger, on a daily basis Ambulance Crews confronted with challenges, Airline Pilots having to make life and death choices in an emergency, Special Forces going into potentially fatal territory. What these individuals share is that they have trained themselves to overcome their initial reactions and instead they:

- ❖ Respond instead of react
- ❖ Take a few moments to gather themselves and remain calm
- ❖ Are smart. They plan, prepare and consider all their options

♦ Learn about assertiveness techniques and the differences between passive behaviour and aggressive behaviour

♦ Given the knowledge that you have gained about different types of bullies, strategically apply appropriate behaviours to your experience of bullying or harassment and know that you can choose your response:

- ❖ In some situations, it may be smart to simply survive the situation, remain neutral, just do your job and keep out of harms way

❖ Some situations can be managed with an assertive response in which you recognise the other person's perspective but in turn express what you do or do not want to happen

❖ Some situations may require that you are firm in your response and it is understood in no uncertain terms that you are saying no

♦ Be thoughtful towards yourself:

❖ If you believe that you have somehow exacerbated a particular situation. Forgive yourself, you are human. Learn from your experience and use it to move forward

❖ Appreciate yourself for handling a challenging period in your life which is now in the past

"Know your own true worth and you shall not perish."

Kahlil Gibran

Part Six. Overcoming the experience of being bullied and harassed

Recovery

Post Traumatic Growth

"No bird soars too high if he soars with his own wings."

William Blake

Post Traumatic Growth

Post traumatic growth refers to the ability to **overcome** and **make sense of** misfortune and suffering.

Post traumatic growth is not only about 'brushing yourself down and brushing things off' but about an opportunity for learning and personal development. You have been changed but you can use your new knowledge to develop foresight, which will serve you well in new situations and enable you to act pre-emptively. Sound judgement will enhance your rational self and wisdom will serve you in future decisions.

Cognitive Dissonance

Having gone through the ordeal of bullying and harassment you will have likely experienced **Cognitive Dissonance.** This means that the beliefs and values you once held about others and about the world have been turned upside down. The beliefs that you held about yourself have been challenged. Prior to going through the situation of bullying/harassment you may have predicted that you would have behaved differently.

Whenever cognitive dissonance occurs it creates an internal motivation to change. This means that sometimes when people have been bullied they take the position *'If you can't beat them join them!'* You are going through a period of putting your self-perception back into harmony. Reading a books like this is one way of helping while you work out why you made certain choices and the influences upon you.

Cognitive Dissonance: Shame and Guilt

During the period of being bullied and harassed

the bully played on a powerful ploy namely, denial, and the knowledge that often the truth daren't be spoken. You were humiliated and placed in a position of vulnerability. The bully relied on you:

- Being ashamed of bringing the bullying into the open

- Thinking that you were the only one who was going through the misery and should have been getting on with life like everyone else, particularly in these days where corporate life reminds us that we should be positive and we are fed a daily diet of social media 'feel-good' slogans

- Fearing that no one would believe you

- Feeling guilt that you had brought the bullying/harassment upon yourself

- Putting up the pretence that nothing was happening

- Being fearful not to confront the situation due to concerns about the consequences
- Playing things down

The bully relied on the organisation, managers, teams and others as:

- Treating the obvious situation as 'The Elephant in the Room'
- Being frightened to do anything for fear of the fallout. For example, legal action or unearthing a 'can of worms' and exposing a deeper problem

Your journey of recovery began when you started to reclaim your power by taking action. Recovery is also to be found in the knowledge that you now know that the feelings and conditions that you experienced were legitimate and real.

Free yourself from the bully/harasser by losing your guilt, shame and humiliation. **Do not accept the 'gifts' of guilt, shame and humiliation.** You do not need to hang onto these emotions. If you have become preoccupied with these feelings, ask in what way they are serving you on your path of recovery and learning. See things for what they were.

Working through Change

Most likely while being so vulnerable and going through this episode in your life you have felt that it could only be happening to you. This has been a period of change, challenging your world and your view of how things should be. Elisabeth Kubler-Ross created a model to describe the experience of change with respect to bereavement. The steps she developed have been applied to many situations and are relevant to understanding your experience of bullying/harassment.

- ♦ **Shock and Denial**
  - ❖ With no experience of bullying, is confused and bewildered and so keeps soldiering on
  - ❖ Try's to rationalise it and just brush it off
  - ❖ Makes jokes about the behaviour
  - ❖ Try's to take a casual approach to the behaviour
  - ❖ *'This can't be happening to me'*

- ♦ **Anger**
  - ❖ *'I don't care, let them get on with it!'*
  - ❖ *'I'm not being driven out. I'll leave when I want to leave!'*

- ♦ **Bargaining (If only...)**
  - ❖ *'If only I don't draw attention to it, it*

will go away'

❖ *If only I work harder/produce better results it will stop'*

♦ **Depression**

    ❖ *'I can't take any more of this, I'm too tired'*

    ❖ Taking stock of the situation

    ❖ Reaching rock bottom (which can become the springboard needed to move forward)

♦ **Acceptance**

    ❖ Accepting the reality of the situation

    ❖ Recovery and healing

    ❖ Learning

The trauma of bullying/harassment

Bullying and harassment can leave you stuck on the process of change or leave you with feelings of anxiety. Other problems can be:

- Distress caused by triggers such as sounds, sights and smells associated with the bullying experience

- Avoidance tactics may be used to dodge anything associated with the bullying/harassment

- Attempts are made to avoid painful thoughts and feelings

- Disrupted sleep patterns and even nightmares

- Loss of concentration

- Loss of interest (*can't be bothered...'*)

You may find it useful to reinterpret your experience. If you are having long term problems, you should seek professional help.

Part Six. Overcoming the experience of being bullied and harassed

Recovery

Rebuilding Confidence

"*Never, never, never, give up.*"

Winston Churchill

Be your own best friend

People are very good at getting stuck in ways of thinking and behaving, quickly forming habits. During the stages of bullying, you not only received messages from the bully and others but you are likely to given yourself negative messages about your own inadequacy *'It was my fault, I brought it on myself' 'I'm not good enough to get another job'*. In addition, we can be our own worst enemy, telling ourselves that things ought to be like this or ought to be like that, when in reality the complexities of life mean that sometimes the nature of things are out of our control. What you can do is acknowledge this understanding, while also giving yourself positive self-affirmations and do this on a daily basis:

- *'I am a valuable person'*
- *'I am capable'*
- *'I am wise'*

- ◆ *'I am strong'*

- ◆ *'I like me'*

Strengthen your self-belief

Reinstate and reinforce your own self-awareness.

Start a notebook record and include the following:

- ◆ A page of what is good about being you

- ◆ A page about the positive ways in which others who like you would describe you

- ◆ A page of all the people to whom you are connected. (For while you may have felt isolated, your network is probably wider than you think)

- ◆ Lists (relating to all facets of your life) with respect to:

  - ❖ Your strengths
  - ❖ All of your achievements
  - ❖ All of the skills you possess
  - ❖ Your qualifications

❖ The places you have been, the things that you have done

❖ The happy times that you have enjoyed

❖ The things you are proud of having accomplished

❖ Set realistic goals for the positive things you are going to do in the future

♦ Create a Gratefulness Journal and record those things you feel grateful for each day and/or the successes you have achieved

♦ Give yourself some 'quick wins'. For example:

❖ Review and tidy up your CV

❖ Refresh your surroundings by de-cluttering, rearranging rooms and furniture or re-decorating

❖ Broaden your horizons a little. Try

doing something fun that you haven't done before such as going to the cinema and seeing a film that you wouldn't normally watch

❖ Do some studying

❖ Plan a trip to somewhere that you have always wanted to visit

♦ Find support from others. Enjoy time with those people who strengthen you and believe in you. Limit your precious time with those people who have a negative effect upon your overall wellbeing

♦ Invest in yourself perhaps by:

❖ Undertaking meditation classes

❖ Connecting with specialist networks and groups

❖ Reading and using self-help books and resources

♦ Recognise in life things don't always go as

we want them to:

❖ Those experiences that we experience as failure or knocks are difficulties to be overcome or to go around, not to blight the rest of your life. In retrospect, a new reality can sometimes be an opportunity

❖ Turn up the controls on your optimistic self and see what is good in the world. Negativity is self-limiting and will inhibit your propensity for pursuing goals, building positive relationships and saying yes to the opportunities which may come your way

❖ Recognise that you may not be able to control everything that happens to you but you can control how you think about what is happening

"Resentment is like drinking poison and then hoping it will kill your enemies."

Nelson Mandela

Part Six. Overcoming the experience of being bullied and harassed

Learning

Empowerment and refocus

"I am not what happened to me, I am what I choose to become."

Carl Jung

'Lose the crutches'

While going through such a difficult time you may have used eating, drinking, excessive viewing of the TV, spending, etc. as 'sticking plasters' to get yourself through. You are healing, now is the time to wean yourself off of these crutches. Engage in activities as previously described, perhaps get involved in charitable works or campaigns, restore healthy sleep patterns and if you can, have a holiday.

Rational Thinking

In life we are constantly learning lessons. We have an experience, are able to reflect upon it, theorise and draw conclusions and apply our learning to new experiences. This period in your life has been just one particular experience. Given current retirement ages, the span of working life can be expected to be about 50 years plus. Wherever you are on the timeline, rationalise the experience by asking how many times it has happened before and what are the chance of it happening again. You are not defined by this event but you have grown in knowledge and understanding.

Detachment

Changing yourself in terms of your outlook and understanding:

- ♦ Detachment is about refocussing your mind and stopping yourself from focussing your emotions and feelings towards the bully/harasser. Ask yourself why you need to keep hold of these feelings? You have control for your minute by minute choices in terms of where you invest your thoughts. Invest them in being the best you can be, in the people that matter and on those things that bring a sense of purpose and joy

♦ While retaining your humanity, you can objectify the bully/harasser and see that whatever you might have done to change the individual(s) in question, it is unlikely that there would have been an alteration in their disposition. Accept that this is how the person was/is. You now understand what was happening. As discussed previously, most likely you were simply the latest target

♦ Your expectations of how people should behave has been given a blow and re-shaped. In future, (while not becoming cynical) adjust your expectations and work within these parameters

Finally, let go of what has happened. Decide what is truly important and what you really want in your life and for the future. *Good Luck!*

Important Note

This book is not a legal handbook or a procedural guide. Any reference to legislation is provided as an overview and should not be read as a statement of law. Relevant Acts are continuously reviewed and revised to be fit for purpose and for our time. Therefore, you should consult appropriate organisations and professional bodies for the most up to date legal advice and information.

This book is about exploring behaviour, the consequences of behaviour and promoting positive steps. This book **should not** be treated as a substitute for organisational policy, procedure or advisory materials.

To the Point

About the Author

Jacqueline Mansell Chartered FCIPD., FSET., is a Chartered Psychologist and business owner who has worked in a career dedicated to learning and development.

During the course of her career Jacqueline has reached many people through her work and interventions, and is now bringing her accumulated knowledge and expertise to a wider audience through her handbooks.

To the Point handbooks have been designed by Jacqueline to provide a compilation of her reference notes and presentation materials, built over the span of many years. The handbooks cover psychological themes accessible and applicable to everyday living.

To the Point

Printed in Great Britain
by Amazon

54335714R00139